Memory Box

Sasha Cerino

BookLeaf Publishing

India | USA | UK

Presentation by *BookLeaf Publishing*

Web: www.bookleafpub.com

E-mail: info@bookleafpub.com

ISBN: 9789357445900

First edition 2022

DEDICATION

dedicating this to all the wandering imperfect
perfect souls out there. you are not alone.

ACKNOWLEDGE
MENT

I acknowledge that I live on the unceded land of the Coast Salish peoples–Sḵwx̱wú7mesh (Squamish), Stó:lō and Səl̓ílwətaʔ/Selilwitulh (Tsleil-Waututh) and xʷməθkʷəy̓əm (Musqueam) Nations. I understand that the indeginous people have been on this land long before any colony has stepped foot upon it. This land has always been and is theirs. Acknowledging that is a start, but more needs to be done when it comes to reconciliation and healing of their people. As a settler, I recognize that I have a privilege and therefore a responsibility to decolonize myself as well as the system at hand that continues to disrupt their humanity. Which is why I stand by and support the indeginous community's right to protest in any form necessary to them.

Making Lumpia

it's funny how the simple act of pulling apart the
wrapper sheets
pull apart the time that has past

suddenly
I am a child once again
in the kitchen
helping mama with dinner

the harmonious chopping of vegetables
bell pepper
green onion
garlic
carrot

a symphony of sounds that feed the insatiable
hunger of feeling at home
no words actually escape our mouth
our synchronized movement
is the communication
it is our dialogue

we then seasoneour filling generously with
soy sauce
garlic powder

salt
pepper

just like how we generously season
the family events and friend gatherings
with laughter
silly shenanigans
cheesy games
and sharing stories

all enveloped together into a package
for another memory to savour afterwards

Mirrors All Around

people are mirrors
reflecting all off one another

the darkest shadows beneath their
hidden cave of locked up skeletons

or their iridescent bright glass palaces
showcasing the grandiose of dreams

or the many mellow lit rooms where familiarity
and content sit

a constant movement between realms
a mirroring of a mirror
an oversaturation of light

it can be blinding
it can be distracting
but always revealing

consciously or unaware

Endless Route

soften hues of blue seats and yellow handles
inside a hollow hexagon
a dark center contrasted by
stark white streak lights
glowing
on and off
lined up like a pathway as if it were to ready to
take flight
hushed passengers existing in their own world
exhausted by their past selves
they all knew that the destination was home
but the journey felt like a timeless drift

Bruised Boundaries

careful
watch your step
the lines breath deep

tensions rise
in unspoken speech

Burning Gasoline

you wriggle in
your sweet nothings
so I stay

but

not after the constant slurs
of always being less then
that I start to believe
I am nothing

I tried to talk to you
about your actions
that heed danger

only to be told that I'm a liar
because you never set anything
on fire

but I watched you pour the gasoline
and see the used matchsticks
in your back pocket

you are the guilty arsonist

blue heart necklace

blue heart necklace
flattered when I got you
my cheeks couldn't have been
a more brighter red

blue heart necklace
so simple
yet so beautiful
I couldn't help but stare

blue heart necklace
I wore you everyday
cause nothing was more true
than the love I felt from you

blue heart necklace
we went to see movies
ate at restaurants
or stayed at his house

blue heart necklace
do you still remember
when it was all good?
it's all a blurr now

blue heart necklace
he betrayed me
he was suppose to be my security
but instead became the intruder

blue heart necklace
I've been crying so much
my tears are long gone
I've turned my feelings on mute

blue heart necklace
it's been years now
and I have stowed you away in a box
as a token

but you are no longer the jewelry I wear

empty jar

why don't you believe me?
you hold what you carry
no matter how contained

you will bleed and drown

gasping for air

scab
scar

burning, it will remain

breathe once more
but shall there be oxygen in my lungs?
or will it be filled to the brim with tired eyes and
repeating channels?

Lost my compass

Seeking help is hard for me
it's like admitting defeat
treason against what I've been told
taught to stand my ground
independent
manage on your own

yet in ways
my hand was still being held
guiding me through a walkway

maybe held too tight at times
blood circulation was lost
the zinging sensation traveling from my fingers
to my arms

but letting go would be more scary
to be left behind
to be lost
or worst of all
fall and never be able to find home

the fickle irony
of ending up deserted anyway
even though I was doing what I was told

and I can't stand my ground if there's no
foundation to be hold
crumbled withered soil

it needs to be tended
cared for
renewed
I can't do it on my own

I need help that will lead myself
home

Moon Fairy

paper mache boats
sailing in the sea of
glow in the dark stars

waiting to see if the girl with
the crescent shaped mark
on her cheek
will arrive

for she is the one
that keeps their beloved
treasures
safe and unharmed

the protector
the guardian
of memories
new and old

giving it back
only when the tide is quiet
and their hearts are open to recieve

once each request is finished
she bows

her head almost touching the ground

and before the night almost turns to day
she vanishes out of sight
leaving behind dust of pure starlight

Foolish Narrator

not again
oh please not again
you're starting to create these stories
out of nothing again

a fantasy that inhabits your mind
a mirage so alluring
it invites you to slow dance with it
in it's chandeleir lit ballroom
marble floor
large glass windows
overlooking a garden

an orchestra to set the mood
as he stands across the room
his eyes wander
until he meets yours-

STOP
wake up
for what you see in front of you
is nothing more than a boy

you're at a party
small talk

playful banter
there is intimacy between friends
 no romance at all

a friend among friends
nothing more
nothing more

leave it at that

don't dawdle in this illusion that only exists in
your head

because then your heart

 starts to believe the fairytale
and that's when the danger is real

heartbreak at the end of that deal

Dear little fishes

hello little fishes
how are you doing today?
you seem to be having some fun
in your little glass case

you've been fed
and your tank has been kept clean
life for you seems
peaceful
serene

but I wonder sometimes
if you ever dream
about what's outside
like do you ever think
is there more to this?

I'd say some of you do
as you jump out
but that only ever ends up
with you underground
in a shoebox this time
buried not too far down

which makes me question further

risking all that for what?
a chance for the big ocean maybe?
unlimited space to swim
so many other fishes to meet

but what if the ocean isn't meant for you?

the rest of you
seem to like going around in circles
cycle after cycle
okay living in your tank
okay with being catered to
okay with the fish
already in your bubble

but I guess each fish
has their own struggles

Unwelcomed at the dinner table

told to eat more until
told to eat less

told to eat
even when I'm full

told not to eat
even when I'm hungry

there's never a time where full meant I enjoyed
my meal
without swallowing the sharp rigid edges of
broken glass

fed to me by hands of one but seemed to expand
when a gathering of people were to exchange a
few words
a few glances

and starving meant being chained to a tick
ticking clock as it's heavy echoes murmur in my
brain

contrasted with a stagnant image of a body that I
outgrew years ago, and this ghostly yearning
arises

clickclickclickclickclick

like a never ending film projector replaying the
same scene, over and over again

buds of unhealed wounds

they say "tough love!"
but tough love is not what I need sometimes,
you know?

tough love has planted the seed of fear

tough love said my emotions are invalid
tough love said I won't support your dreams at
all because thats not what I envisioned for you
"that's not realistic"
tough love said I care more about your "success"
than your well being

tough love told me.
has made me believe.
that
"the truth is, I am not worthy unless I have
achieved accolades"
"to be the best"
"to work hard"

without ever thinking

to stop and ask
"are you doing okay?"
"anything I can do to help?"
"hey, why don't we rest for a bit?"
allow some breathing room
to refresh
to unwind

but no

"productivity" over humanity

tough love was me having a full on break down
only for you to pat my back, and say "get
stronger"
"this will make you stronger"
when all I ever wanted
just for a single moment,
is to be cradled
to be held gently
and to be whispered
"there, there
let it all out
I'll be here as long as you need,
I love you no matter what"

is that too much to ask?
am I asking for too much?

A shot of Covid and mental illness

getting up is the biggest chore

when painting and drawing are no longer my
muses anymore

daunting dentist appointment
transiting alone

rain or sunshine
I still feel numb

a hollowness of the endless dark void

sleep paralysis is reoccurring
paranoid about whether the noises are real

and the creeping of a shadow, is it actually
there?

when will I feel safe?
when will being an adult become fun?

I feel so behind

cleaning is a form of control

but where has my energy gone?
my bed is messy
dust on the tables and shelves
and there is hair all over my floor

will I ever return to the normal I knew before?

Drawing Thoughts

a property of drawing is the permanence it
leaves

a documentation of where your mind was going

a retracing of steps when you look back

or realizations of what you have done
revealing nuisances

practice takes forms in my small sketchbooks
tiny doodles that line the notes
of my lecture classes
the paintings that take space
in my room

an exploration of material
and pacing
of how my thoughts move

Temptation Cheats

leave the wishes to the bones
for no one knows where the pockets of unsaid
cries hide

"the flame is not hot!"

don't touch it
don't touch it
don't touch it
don't touch it

AAAAAAHHH

you lied.

Too Much Static

tendencies of shutting down when the T.V gets
loud
the room gets quiet
and the remote
is nowhere to be found

Expanding Bubbles

critical thinking
unproblematic doing
performative activism
hoarding billionares
marginalized groups of people

intersectionality
phobias
narratives
superiority
discussions

mistakes are the inevitable
but accountability needs to be served
when someone becomes above the law
following rules will become absurd

connection in community
trust is sacred
respect is a ritual to uphold

when broken
time after time again
many fires will start
and will continue to unfold

the world is big enough for everyone
yet space is limited because of one very few
individuals
a system built only to favour white ideals

our first step
to change
to rewrite
unlearn and learn
decolonize
from top to bottom

www.ingramcontent.com/pod-product-compliance
Lightning Source LLC
LaVergne TN
LVHW021332200726
843509LV00014B/2497